First World War
and Army of Occupation
War Diary
France, Belgium and Germany

51 DIVISION
153 Infantry Brigade,
Brigade Trench Mortar Battery
1 March 1916 - 31 August 1916

WO95/2882/4

Published by

The Naval & Military Press Ltd

Unit 10 Ridgewood Industrial Park,

Uckfield, East Sussex,

TN22 5QE England

Tel: +44 (0) 1825 749494

www.naval-military-press.com

www.nmarchive.com

This diary has been reprinted in facsimile from the original. Any imperfections are inevitably reproduced and the quality may fall short of modern type and cartographic standards.

© Crown Copyright
Images reproduced by permission of The National Archives, London, England, 2015.

Contents

Document type	Place/Title	Date From	Date To
Heading	WO95/2882/4 Brigade Trench Motar Battery		
Heading	51st Division 153rd Trench Mortar Bty 1916 Mar Aug 1916		
Heading	March 1916 153/1 Trench Mortar Battery Vol 1		
War Diary	Cardonette	01/03/1916	06/03/1916
War Diary	Fienvillers	07/03/1916	09/03/1916
War Diary	Doullens Ivergny	10/03/1916	12/03/1916
War Diary	Maroeuil Trenches	13/03/1916	13/03/1916
War Diary	Trenches	14/03/1916	31/03/1916
Heading	War Diary 153rd Trench Mortar Battery From 1st July 1916 To 31st July 1916 Volume 24		
War Diary	Trenches	01/07/1916	20/07/1916
War Diary	Mametz Wood	21/07/1916	26/07/1916
War Diary	High Wood	26/07/1916	31/07/1916
War Diary	Becordel	01/08/1916	01/08/1916
War Diary	Meaulte	06/08/1916	06/08/1916
War Diary	Mericourt Longpre	09/08/1916	11/08/1916
War Diary	Racquinghem	16/08/1916	16/08/1916
War Diary	Armentieres	17/08/1916	17/08/1916
War Diary	Trenches	18/08/1916	31/08/1916

WO95/2682/4

Brigade Trench Mortar Battery

51ST DIVISION

153RD TRENCH MORTAR BTY
1916 MAR ~~JLY~~-AUG 1916

WAR DIARY
or
INTELLIGENCE SUMMARY.

Army Form C. 2118.

March 1916

153/1 Trench Mortar Battery

WAR DIARY
or
INTELLIGENCE SUMMARY

Army Form C. 2118.

Place	Date	Hour	Summary of Events and Information	Remarks and references to Appendices
Cardonnette	1/3/16	5 p.m.	No officer H/Q 117th Trench Mortar Battery (3.7") report to my duty. I report to my Brigade (153 Infantry) for duty. I proceed to H/Q of Battery. Strength is the Hy. T.M. Battery representing the Brigade. The Battery is allotted billets in this area. Commence the training and organization of the Battery. The organization so far more intensive and difficult.	# Battery Strength 4/2 offrs. 1 Sergt. 4 Cpls.
Do.	2/3/16		My working programme for the Battery consists of "Gun Drill", practical notes on working and laying of Guns, and "Care of Matério"; Rifle & Kit Inspections.	5/16 gunners sends
Do.	3/3/16		Am falling out myself greatly with training. The men advertised to on the 3.7" and Stokes Mortars. This day inspect the "Alexander Jun Brake" a recent. accepting T.M. invented by Major Alexander, who is 1/6th Black Watch (Q.H.S.). It has a 2 lb Cordite and is fired by means of a Nobels Sporting Cartridge. So effective is the recoil resistance of the Mortar that it can be fired off the knee. It's weight is 80 lbs. The principle of this Mortar is working is a good reason why its acceptance of the gun free. A the field of Trench Mortars there is no scope for improvement and organisation of design. Saw entries to God. check much needed today; that officers of which would make labour and money saving.	20 offrs. & men als
Do.	5/3/16		Attend Divine Service with Bttry. Snow fall all the evening. Received orders to leave Bgde. Hqrs. at 2 a.m. alongst Battalion representatives for the trenches. N. of Arras which we are to take over.	

Army Form C. 2118.

WAR DIARY
or
INTELLIGENCE SUMMARY.
(Erase heading not required.)

Place	Date	Hour	Summary of Events and Information	Remarks and references to Appendices
Cardonnette	6/3/16	2 a.m.	Leave Bgh. Hq by M.T. Bngde. the Trench Mortar arms Divisions been Evacuation at 10 a.m. having reported at Bgade (First) Hqrs at Mamets. Proceed to Bronfaut Farm, Up Bryan Trench running near Faire to Somme Bychyn. These are noted to Hqrs of Trench Mortar officer. He made himself acquainted with all his dispositions on the high ground on either ridges, the guns were 580 yds/ye. Methods there appeared to be good, most lighthearted. He had an implement in all dug-outs and ammunition stores are suitably placed by guns.	
		4 p.m.	Return to new billeting area at Fresnillers Ampie 1 off. Receive orders from Front. Won't T.M. School at Volkerenne the Scheme for question of a Stokes Bryant Captain Hutson OC school.	
	8/3/16		Visit of our T.M. school Two interior Stokes & Short Mortars due to shell cartridge continue opening in making off from shell bore.	
Do.	9/3/16		March to Doullens. Billeted the there.	
Doullens	10/3/16		March to Gezincy.	
Gezincy	11/3/16		In rest.	
	12/3/16		March to Mamot a distance of 18 Kilos. Arrive 7.30 p.m.	

Army Form C. 2118.

WAR DIARY
or
INTELLIGENCE SUMMARY.
(Erase heading not required.)

Instructions regarding War Diaries and Intelligence Summaries are contained in F. S. Regs., Part II. and the Staff Manual respectively. Title pages will be prepared in manuscript.

Place	Date	Hour	Summary of Events and Information	Remarks and references to Appendices
Reserve Trenches	13/3/16		Visit again in line trench T.M. Offrs. Unsatis. that there are two gun positions – Pos.1 2nds) with two alternate emplacements. Intermediate post unsatis. Post Chanot unsatis. Reserve	
			Magazine of Pri. plats. adrange of Batties.	
Trenches	14/3/16	6 p.m.	Whitt Battery took up position in the Red. Instruct N.C.O's on field [?]. Much street retaliation in response of rifle grenades	
Do	15/3/16		manouvres. Fire on Ralpho's fort for Salvos attempting. Found it is possible to put the afternoon for. Hefeton fires above the fires of the enemy. Receive this morning 340 additional rds of 3.7" ammunition.	
Do.	16/3/16		Fire in enemy saphead. T.M. shells are retaken. Enemy's T.M. shell appears to correspond to our 4" T.M. Shells not weights about 8 lbs. Try fire by Rumour. Practice against snipe posts and enemy working party. Enemy reply with	
	17/3/16	10 p.m.	rifle explosive and incendiary [?] This day we sent 451 Batty Councill (2°T.M.B.) received a third-few batteries on Qents. Drawing notice of they are retaliating pressures the respondents both for need, his for destructive effect.	

Confidential.

War Diary
of
153rd Trench Mortar Battery.

From 1st July 1916 to 31st July 1916.

Volume 2.

Vol V

WAR DIARY or INTELLIGENCE SUMMARY

Army Form C. 2118.
No. 30927/A
153 T.M. Bty.
HIGHLAND DIV

Place	Date	Hour	Summary of Events and Information	Remarks and references to Appendices
Trenches	1/11/16		Action of mortars in trenches stationary. Enemy fires over 5 or 6 types of mortars on this sector of the heavy type mainly "Erin's sausage". Few who knew this last day were hit from the enemy, the difficulty of getting as much fire to bear is a slow one from sky. I was taught that this mortar was synonymous behind the lines, any high railway. The location of the gun was definitely hidden more than in one screen concealing mortar from W. Enemy has on more than one occasion concealed mortar from M.2. Sects.	W.
do	10/11/16 to 14/11/16		During this period Stokes mortars were used to put a considerable barrage on trench areas flashing fire of Fred entered by our mapping party from light pens (for concentrates was with flash). 900 rounds fired during the period of bombardment which form all	A.1

Army Form C. 2118.

WAR DIARY
or
INTELLIGENCE SUMMARY
(Erase heading not required.)

Instructions regarding War Diaries and Intelligence Summaries are contained in F. S. Regs., Part II. and the Staff Manual respectively. Title Pages will be prepared in manuscript.

Place	Date	Hour	Summary of Events and Information	Remarks and references to Appendices
Toutencourt	14/7/16		accounts were extremely effective.	
	15/7/16		Battery leaves Toutencourt and moves to Hedauville. On this move is presented specially for the first time the inadequacy of our Battery Transport facilities. Motorcars are found to be not only too slowly built, but also extremely difficult owing to their awkward construction to man-handle or move along at a reasonable pace. If one wishes to be capable to move with an infantry column. Motor transport is finally outsupplies and amounts to the present W.E. impasse.	
	16/7/16 to 20/7/16		Move up to the line by way of Hedauville, Bouzincourt and Mesnil.	
Mesnil Wood	2/7/16		In support on the Trailet of Aug: onto, having relieved the 98th Trench M. Mortar Battery	W.E. A.W.

2449 Wt. W14957/M90 750,000 1/16 J.B.C. & A. Forms/C.2118/12.

WAR DIARY or INTELLIGENCE SUMMARY

Army Form C. 2118.

Place	Date	Hour	Summary of Events and Information	Remarks and references to Appendices
Martin Wood	25/9/16 26/9/16		Enemy bombards frequently vicinity of Martin-pg: outs all night. Slight Gunfire. Casualties in my Battery are slight here in comparison to other units located here.	
High Wood	26/9/16 27/9/16		Take over two guns from 154 Trench Mortar Battery; one emplaced at eastern side of High Wood, the other in a shell-hole in the centre of the wood. A shell-hole found A.16 made quite a good temporary emplacement provided it is deepened. Long-range cartridges were being used. I am ordered to take up two employes my remaining guns in High Wood. This found did not present any great difficulty as the guns were transported by Lewis Carts almost up to High Wood itself across the open. One gun out of action through being hit by shrapnel.	

WAR DIARY
or
INTELLIGENCE SUMMARY

Army Form C. 2118.

Place	Date	Hour	Summary of Events and Information	Remarks and references to Appendices
High Wood	26/7/16		Emplacements. I have little difficulty in deciding upon. Four guns are replaced in an advanced gun-pit, being fired running at a tangent from the Eastern side of High Wood. Three guns I have in shell holes in to the immediate the Switch.	
	27/7/16		Obey bell guns from a searching fire of one immediately behind enemy front trench and in front of his Switch Trench. Sunken Road, Eastern strong point and fortified House in hood are to have special attention. Twelve hundred rounds of ammunition (partly Fuzed) are accumulated at the guns. Carrying parties undertake but available in Eucalthis during the portage of the ammunition.	
	28/7/16		I consider a certain amount of risk was run before the attack itself by no strong ammunition shelters being available other than at Mametz hood and High hood. This risk was traced to a certain extent by ammunition	

Army Form C. 2118.

WAR DIARY
or
INTELLIGENCE SUMMARY
(Erase heading not required.)

Place	Date	Hour	Summary of Events and Information	Remarks and references to Appendices
High Wood	30/11/16		Being distributed as far as possible placed in shell holes. Emplacements improved also ranging completed.	
-do-	30/11/16		Direct searching fire for the most part during the Preliminary bombardment until infantry are well up when guns are ordered to put up a barrage to repel fire. Find difficulty in maintaining liaison with companies attacking. This however, that they are not yet up to barrage lines so renew outbursts of fire. Repeating to push forward Lewis guns along eastern edge of wood. Our second wave of infantry retires however. First wave reported help up. The wounded still with the guns and holes in case of Counter-attack.	
		9.15 p.m.	Our infantry finally fall back to their original line of resistance.	(1)

Place	Date	Hour	Summary of Events and Information	Remarks and references to Appendices
High Wood	31/7/16	5 pm	Handed over seven guns in High Wood to 152 Trench Mortar Battery relieving.	

A. Austin Capt.
Comdg. T.M. Bty
153 T.M. Bty

Place	Date	Hour	Summary of Events and Information	Remarks and references to Appendices
RECORDED	1/8/16			

In honour I instruct officers and other ranks in view of the 35th Div's "North." Casualties had been proportionally high in my Battery during my strenuous action in the General Offensive. I feel whilst my Battery was in action in High Wood on the night of the attack on 30th July I had not a single casualty. This was partly due to the guns being deeply emplaced and always accompanying to the enemy line. But it was necessary to fill up the gaps where to man's personnel in the Battery as quickly as possible. This was done by attaching to Divning intelligent men. In this connection there is a distinct change in the point of view taken up by the Commanding Officers of Batteries. They now could see to my Battery as representing useful men, to actually of advantage factually. Which was denied from the 35th's mortar intelligent men had especially very Capable N.C.Os must be applied. a T.M. Battery I have forced that at most N.C.O. can take full and necessary advantage of the opportunities by training & preparing for staff and Group Junior etc. I now organize my Battery as that Right & Left Sections consist of five gun Each. — all commanded by Officers and each Subaltern L/S. B.C.

A.S.

WAR DIARY or INTELLIGENCE SUMMARY

Army Form C. 2118.

Place	Date	Hour	Summary of Events and Information	Remarks and references to Appendices
MEAULTE	6/8/16		("D") recommended by an N.C.O. This present map is much appreciated by all ranks. Range hard to harness. Have again urged the necessity for adequate transport for Trithis Kung supplies to Battery.	A.M.
MERICOURT	9/8/16	12 P.M.	Entrain.	
LONGPRÉ		5 P.M.	Detrain: March to MARIESSART, 8 mls from LONGPRÉ.	
	11/8/16	2:30 P.M.	Entrain once more, by new means after the return march of eight miles, which seems somewhat after one night's stay in MARIESSART.	
-do-		5 P.M.	After detraining at TIENNES arrive RACQUIN'G 11:45 P.M. Many of my men have developed sore feet.	A.M.
RACQUIN'G HEM.	16/8/16	1:45 P.M.	Leave for EBBEINGHEM STATION.	
		4 P.M.	Entrain for STEENWERKE.	
		5:30 P.M.	Arrive STEENWERKE. Proceed to billets in ARMENTIERES. No litter in this movement. Remained in billets which I find somewhat dirty.	A.M.
ARMENTIÈRES	17/8/16	12 noon	Relieve 2nd New Zealand T.M. Battery.	

1577 Wt. W10791/1773 500,000 1/15 D. D. & L. A.D.S.S./Forms/C. 2118.

WAR DIARY or INTELLIGENCE SUMMARY

Army Form C. 2118.

Place	Date	Hour	Summary of Events and Information	Remarks and references to Appendices
ARMENTIERES	17/8/16		This Battery has been in a slovenly fashion. They appear vague & or registration tables, nothing of guns or trench mainly engaged. I noted myself in types at TISSAGE - D not P?	A.M.
TRENCHES	18/8/16		9 round emplacements of Right Section. These are unfinished for the most part. Prepare to provide overhead cover for them.	
do	19/8/16		9 round emplacements of Left Section. Different experiences is good here & A.M. unfinished. Prepare to provide overhead cover.	A.M.
-do-	20/8/16		Continue to improve defensive positions	
-do-	21/8/16		Scheme of defensive positions completed whereby in case of attack, eight guns of my Battery can turn & enemy's firing and gaps in front line W.L. repelled. Small 'x' scheme engaged on this keeping brought up and held retaliation.	
do	22/8/16		Prepare Offensive action Positions.	
do	23/8/16		Engaged in various offensive actions. Everyone all ? of retaliation S.O.S. in still extraordinarily quickly for no interest. He also retaliates with sausage shaped minenwerfers of 90 lbs or thereabouts.	A.M.

WAR DIARY or INTELLIGENCE SUMMARY

Army Form C. 2118.

Place	Date	Hour	Summary of Events and Information	Remarks and references to Appendices
TRENCHES	28/8/16		Enemy retaliation heavy to our north, slight firing Pom-Pom shells from a slight gun on the village of IRBLINGHIEN. The Sellenu encroachment with gas attack did not take place this night owing to inopportune weather conditions.	A.A.
-do-	29/8/16		Indement weather greatly deprecated the issuability of my scheme. Finds.	A.A.
-do-	31/8/16	1:34 A.M.	heavy T.M. grenade & supplemented by four guns from the 158th Trench Mortar Battery commenced bombardment (as pre-arranged) of enemy line, firing on average four rds per gun per minute.	
		2:20 A.M.	hy guns cease firing. By all accounts the guns ranged very successfully to the enemy limits and our trench-mortars fired immensely effectively. The enemy was certainly handicapped in his retaliation by lack of guns of all types. His retaliation was feeble, consisting for the most part of 77 mm shells. No guns experienced T.M.'s was hit. A great difficulty prevailed itself during the firing of T.M. mortars however, 9" m.w. from that have plates sunk deeply into the	

WAR DIARY
or
INTELLIGENCE SUMMARY.

Army Form C. 2118.

Place	Date	Hour	Summary of Events and Information	Remarks and references to Appendices
TRENCHES	31/5/16		emplacement to during the firing and in some cases almost dis-appears with the sudden changes. This entailed a serious loss of valuable time during the bombardment. Certainly some type of revolver-carrying strong shedding for the rear-blocks must be improvised especially at the width. Conditions are likely to become worse during the winter months. I am reporting to Brigade on the matter and also intend writing to II Army T.M. School on the subject.	

A Hunkin Capt.
Commanding,
183 Trench Mortar Battery

www.ingramcontent.com/pod-product-compliance
Lightning Source LLC
Chambersburg PA
CBHW081508160426
43193CB00014B/2623